SKY,
EARTH,
OTHER

Marian Christie

Published by Penteract Press, 2024

PenteractPress.com

Twitter.com/PenteractPress

Cover and Internal Images by Marian Christie

Design by Marian Christie

Typeset in Palatino Linotype

ISBN 978-1-913421-49-6

FIRST EDITION

for
Bob
our children
and our grandchildren

Introduction

The connection between poetry and mathematical sequencing extends back over millennia. Descriptions of metrical patterns in Sanskrit poetry by Pingala (c. 450 – 200 BCE), Virahanka (c. 700 CE) and Hemachandra (c. 1150 CE) indicate knowledge of the following sequence:

$$1, 1, 2, 3, 5, 8, 13, 21, 34, 55, 89, \ldots.$$

In western mathematics this is known as the Fibonacci sequence, after the 13th century mathematician Leonardo Pisano, whose nickname was Fibonacci. Following the first two terms, each successive term is the sum of the two preceding numbers: so $2 = 1 + 1, 3 = 2 + 1, 5 = 3 + 2$ and so on. The numbers generated in this way are called Fibonacci numbers. The sequence has many mathematical applications, and is associated with certain growth patterns and spiral formations in nature, as well as with the aesthetically pleasing Golden Ratio. It also provides the basis for the Fib, a recognised form in contemporary experimental poetry.

All the poems in this collection are constrained in some way by the Fibonacci sequence or by Fibonacci numbers. In most cases, the Fibonacci structure is defined by either a word or a syllable count per line: exceptions are indicated in the Notes.

Contents

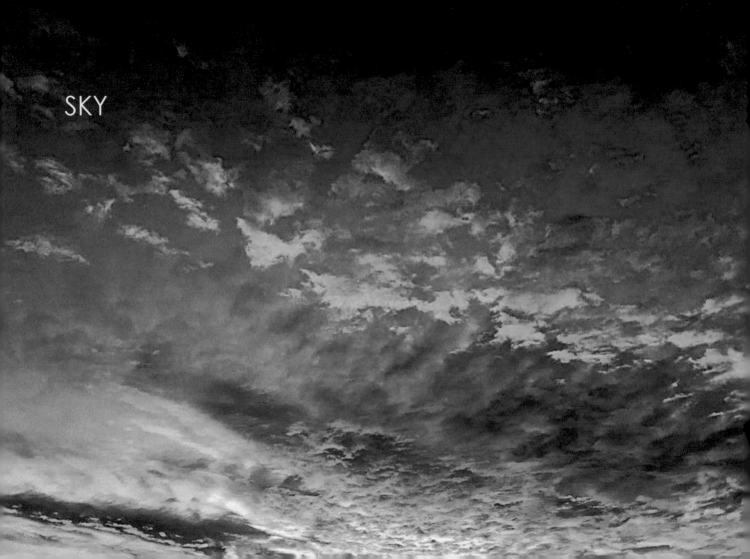

SKY

Clouds

not
spheres
dragons
giant birds
dinosaur footprints
in the sky. Their edges fade, blur
into others, grow
indistinct —
shapeshift
like
us.

Dawn variations

variation 1

quietly
dawns
the day
golden sun arising

copper
clouds
are scattered
over the horizon

variation 2

day
dawns
golden
quietly

horizon
scattered
clouds
sun

variation 3

day
dawns
golden.
copper clouds
quietly scattered.
horizon — the arising sun.

Holding Pattern

Land spreads below like old skin, criss-crossed with fields and trees,
      pale blue veins fading into mist.
          We circle once more,
             look down, see

     pale blue veins. Fading into mist,
        your wicker coffin.
          The elm tree.

      We circle once more.
          Old landmarks
            fade. We

        look down, see
          rushing
              trees —

                 land.

Moonset

wolf
moon
slinks down
to deep clouds

thin-
boned
winter
claws the sky

cloud jewels

lumine

dusk

skies

Venus through the trees

as
if
so close
I could reach
beyond the branches
clasp your radiance in my hands
entice you gently
from the sky
so close
as
if

Voyager 1

Gravity defined your journey's arc; you hitched a ride
past Jupiter, Saturn, strange moons
and shimmering rings.
Last image
looking
back —
Earth.
Home.
But there's
no return.
You must fly, tiny
messenger, beyond our Sun's reach
to roam the Milky Way forever — blind, lost, alone.

when the universe

has stopped

creating

stars

and all reserves of hydrogen

have been

consumed

light

will become

a

rarity

something

to search for

in the cold black sky

as if

there would be

any one

any

being

any

thing

to do the searching

scattered

among

detritus

of lost

planets and

dismembered

galaxies

beyond

grasping
gravity
of black holes

a few embers slowly dimming

when these fade

and matter itself

de-

grades

will   there

still   be

the   faintest

echo

of

beginnings

a   reminder   that

there   was

once

a

birth

EARTH

Self-similarities

cloud iterations
in a cobalt sky — the sea
trembles their shadows

from storm-clouds to earth
lightning splits and splits again
seeks an easy path

fissured limestone cliffs   against flaming sky
define jagged boundaries   trees flaunt winter nakedness
between land and sea   patterns of patterns

bronchial branches   crystalline snowflake   neodymium
within the lobes of the lungs serrated stellar dendrites nickel oxide — quantum scaled
pathways for our breath   glinting fronds of ice   magnetic domains

Pathways

O

I

am

not

going

anywhere

unaccompanied

by life's patterns: a whorl

in a pinecone, branches on oak or elm trees,

the petal count of a daisy, the helix at the heart of a chrysanthemum,

the shell of a nautilus swimming in the ocean. A sequence hides in the shape of probabilities,
and in my own DNA.

Weeds are plants in the wrong place

I
dig
deep. Dock
roots resist,
refusing to yield
to my weeder's clay-probing tines.
Dock, bindweed, brambles belong here, stubborn as the soil

in which acorns transform themselves
into tiny trees —
soil that will
not hold
strange
plants.

Rangelands

sometimes
    blood
oozes viscous
    from the sky

        along a mottled marula branch
           a mother leopard
        has draped
          her
      kill

  all
    that
     is left
  of the river
gouges a wound through sand

            scavengers
         plunder
          abandoned bones

Snake

a green
mamba uncoils from
sleep, slowly slithers
along a branch of the fig tree,
waits for an unsuspecting bulbul to land — then strikes

Snails

A

thin

slime trail

meanders

over the gravel

to my flowerbeds, where hostas

that I had tended so carefully have been reduced

to tattered shreds. A robin perches among panicles of lilac as you approach

with buttered scones and coffee. Light slants through leaves, glistens the slime trail silver.
Everything contributes to the dazzle of this day — even snails.

Cobweb

predator and prey
sticky threads
of thought
bind
us

we
are
enmeshed
in a web
woven by our minds

Seasons

sun
low
days short
shadows long
tilted from the light

tilted to the light
shadows short
days long
sun
high

sun
high
days long
shadows short
tilted to the light

tilted from the light
shadows long
days short
sun

Winter Solstice

Earth holds the hunkering sun close

hugs light through branches

clinging to

this brief

bleak

day.

December rose

leaves

frost-

frozen;

petals red

as arterial

blood, fragile as a baby's heart.

Murmuration

A

bright

crisp dawn —

early frost

glazes hedgerows, ice

jaggedly kaleidoscopes light.

Mist nebulizes over pearly, quiet rivers.

Starling transformations undulate, voluptuous, with xylophonic, yearning zest.

Aubade

First

note

predawn

a song thrush —

then robin, blackbird,

chaffinch, wren. Earth turns, joyfully.

OTHER

Child

I

will

hold you   wrap you

tenderly   in a shawl

cradled in my arms   with warm gentle words

keep you safe   protect you

from storms

from

pain

Post lockdown

Let

us

uncurl

carefully

from our aloneness

like fragile shoots that, warmed by spring,

open to the light. Let us be gentle with our smiles,

be tender with our touch. For who knows the sadness that has petrified inside our hearts?

Absences

it
is
not death,
fathomless
beside my bed, but
the absence of death, the *before*,
lurching incrementally towards an ellipsis….
….like an absence of clouds at the closing down of day
when all colour slowly leaches
from the sky, yielding
to stars, cold,
soundless
as
snow

riff

wind

winded
       deadwind   headwind
windchill   windswept   windshear
    upwind   downwind   crosswind
      windbreak   windborne

windchime

          windy

windy

    winder   winding
wind-along   wind-through   wind-around

wind-down   wind-up   side-wind
            unwind   rewind

winding-sheet

                    wound

   wound

        wounding   wounder
open-wound   closed-wound   dressed-wound
        woundless   war-wound   knife-wound
            head-wound   death-wound

                    wounded

   ~~win~~*dead*

And for the rest of time

I
don't
recall
my falling.
One moment I was
standing at the edge, admiring
the view — then my foot must have slipped
          on the age-smoothed rock
                I tumbled
                  into the ravine
                  helpless
                      fragmented
                      and
                        alone
                      with
                          no
                          way
                          out

Pandora

do
  not
    open
          the casket,
    child — do not release
its secret contents to the world

red shoes

red

shoes

red shoes

take this gift

of red shoes   they will

teach you how to dance   they will make

you dance all day   they will make you dance all night   in red

shoes dance the fields dance the hills   dance the far side of the moon   dance the
stars   dance till they kill....

please
please
please

STOP
STOP
STOP
STOP

shouting
shouting
shooting

WE

MUST

LISTEN

CAREFULLY

WHEN

WE

BOTH MAKE

A HALF TURN

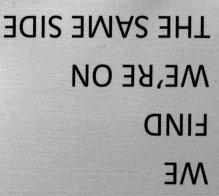

THE SAME SIDE

WE'RE ON

FIND

WE

Foothills

We
saw
two men
that morning
drinking espresso
in small thick cups at a table
of chipped formica, beneath a lime tree by the edge
of the village square. The heat was in the air, not the coffee, which they contemplated
in silence as their fathers had before them, brushing
away flies while war unravelled
on the other side
of dark peaks
where bears
still
roam.

All night we heard them

All night we heard them throbbing the darkness
    as searchlights tunnelled the woods,
        the wind relentless.
            We hid

as searchlights tunnelled — the woods
    hugging our silence,
        ravaged by

the wind. Relentless
    images besieged
        us.

We hid
    beliefs —
        bodies.

View no fiery night

No

one

went to

the tower

to vie with the foe.

Fretting, worn, we rove in night fog —

the ring, the theft, the vow forgotten. Hovering high

over the town, the frightening wyvern, whirr of her winging interwoven with fire.

Spaces in between

we   walk

the   path

      side   by   side

          our   hands   not   touching

             careful   to   avoid   the   spaces   between

                 words   we   dare   not

                    say   places   we

                        dare   not

                        yet   go

Riddle

I

am

perfect.

I'm the sum

of Fibonacci

numbers. Find me here – who am I?

Tree clambering

mysteries wait patiently to be revealed as we contemplate questions to which we have not yet found answers

in the unbounded tree of our imagination

among branches

found

am

I

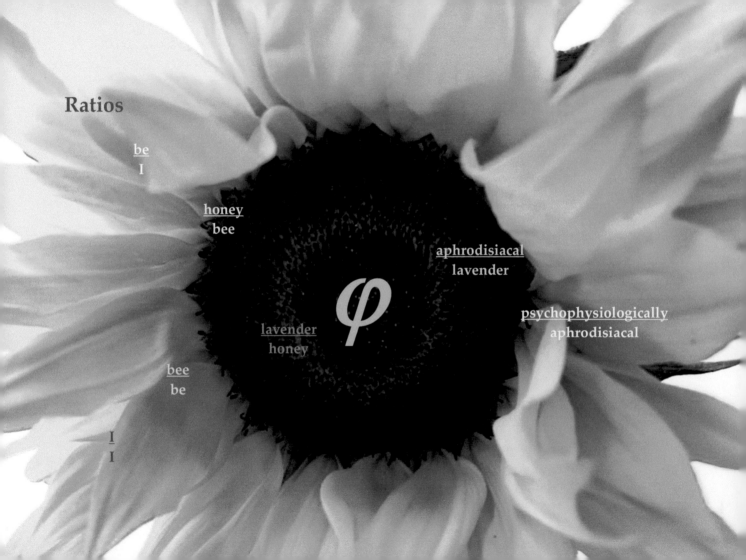

Ratios

$$\frac{be}{I}$$

$$\frac{honey}{bee}$$

$$\frac{aphrodisiacal}{lavender}$$

$$\frac{psychophysiologically}{aphrodisiacal}$$

$$\frac{lavender}{honey}$$

$$\varphi$$

$$\frac{bee}{be}$$

$$\frac{I}{I}$$

In the field

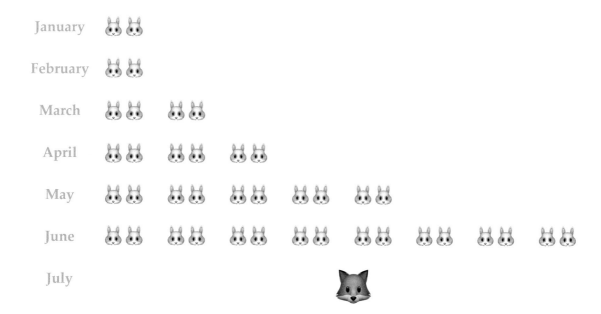

January 🐰🐰

February 🐰🐰

March 🐰🐰 🐰🐰

April 🐰🐰 🐰🐰 🐰🐰

May 🐰🐰 🐰🐰 🐰🐰 🐰🐰 🐰🐰

June 🐰🐰 🐰🐰 🐰🐰 🐰🐰 🐰🐰 🐰🐰 🐰🐰 🐰🐰

July 🦊

The Timeless Test of 1939

Coin

spun —

Melville

won the toss.

"Camp on the wicket,"

he told his team, and so they did,

batting over four days (including a day of rest).

England's first innings was equally grim, grinding out runs on a flat-rolled pitch. Boredom

prevailed in the Durban sun. Day followed wearisome day. Yet more runs, more bowlers' despair, punctuated by rain and a second rest day

as the timeless Test sauntered towards a conclusion. According to the rules, one side had to win. South Africa or England? An outcome dangled enticingly. But it rained again, and the English team had a boat to catch….

On the squash court

we

dance

around

each other

as we have always

done — mindful of red lines, mindful

of each other's space, acknowledging our sweet returns,

intensive rallies, winning shots. And the score doesn't matter. It is always love all.

Writing to constraints

bind

words

tightly

together

observe how

patterns

take

shape

Notes on the poems

Dawn variations. Three rearrangements of my first poem, which was written when I was five:

> Quietly dawns the day
> golden sun arising.
> Copper clouds are scattered
> over the horizon.

Holding Pattern combines a Fibonacci structure (by syllable count) with a variation of the trimeric form.

The shape of *Voyager 1* is defined by a hyperbola.

Degeneration consists of random fragments from the Fibonacci sequence. Each line contains a Fibonacci number by both word and syllable count (not necessarily the same).

Self-similarities is a fractal poem. The Fibonacci structure is defined by the number of stanzas per row.

Pathways is a Fibonacci poem by letter count. In addition, the number of letters comprising each word is a Fibonacci number.

Murmuration is an abecedarian.

Child can be read down the left side, down the right side, as well as horizontally line by line.

Red Shoes contains only monosyllabic words.

We must listen carefully and *When we both make a half turn* are Möbius strip poems.

All night we heard them is a combination of a Fibonacci structure (by word count) and a trimeric.

View no fiery night is a sequential lipogram; each line only contains letters that form the corresponding Fibonacci number (respectively one, one, two, three, five, eight, thirteen, twenty-one), as well as the letters of any preceding numbers in the sequence.

Spaces in between. The Fibonacci structure is determined by the number of spaces between words per line.

Riddle. A perfect number is a positive integer that is equal to the sum of its positive divisors, excluding the number itself. The answer is 6 (= 3 + 2 + 1).

Tree clambering is inspired by the Markov tree, a technique for obtaining solutions to the Markov equation $x^2 + y^2 + z^2 = 3xyz$, where x, y and z are positive integers. Solutions (which occur in triples) are known as Markov numbers. In one of mathematics' many beautiful relationships, every second number in the Fibonacci sequence is also a Markov number, i.e. 1, 2, 5, 13, 34, 89…. This is indicated by the number of letters in each line of the poem (89, 34, 13, 5, 2 and 1 respectively). The poem may be read from the top down, or from the bottom up.

Ratios. The golden ratio, represented in mathematics by the Greek letter phi (φ), is an irrational number that has many interesting mathematical and aesthetic properties, and can be found in certain patterns in nature, such as the arrangement of seeds in a sunflower. Its value is given by

$$\varphi = \frac{1+ \sqrt{5}}{2} = 1.61803 \text{ .... (to 5 decimal places)}$$

The poem illustrates the fact that the ratio of consecutive Fibonacci numbers converges to φ. Here the Fibonacci numbers are represented by the number of letters in each word.

In the field is a visual representation of a problem investigated by Fibonacci in 1202. A pair of rabbits (one male, one female) in a walled field are mature enough to breed after one month, producing a similar pair at the end of the following month. Assuming the breeding pattern continues in this way, how many pairs of rabbits will be in the field after one year? (Fibonacci's model did not consider the possibility that a fox might jump over the wall.)

The Timeless Test of 1939 describes the longest game of Test cricket ever played, between South Africa and England in Durban from 3rd — 14th March 1939. The rules of cricket have since been changed; nowadays the duration of a Test match is limited to a maximum of five days.

Writing to constraints. There are shifting patterns in the sequence of vowels.

Versions of the following poems have been previously published.

- *Pathways* was first published in **Independent Variable** (2018)
- *Voyager 1, Snails, All night we heard them, Post Lockdown, And for the rest of time* and *Weeds are plants in the wrong place* were all originally published in **The Fib Review**.
- *Riddle* and *Aubade* were published in **The Journal of Humanistic Mathematics** (2022).
- *Holding Pattern* was published in **14 Magazine** (Vanguard Editions, 2023).
- *Snake* was published in **Periodicity Journal** (2023)

Marian Christie is from Harare, Zimbabwe. She lived in various countries in Africa, Europe and the Middle East before moving to her present home in southeast England.

Publications include *Fractal Poems* and *Triangles*, both with Penteract Press, and a collection of essays, *From Fibs to Fractals: exploring mathematical forms in poetry*. She is co-editor of *Tesserae: a mosaic of poems by Zimbabwean women*, published by Carnelian Heart.

Marian blogs at www.marianchristiepoetry.net and is on X/Twitter @marian_v_o.